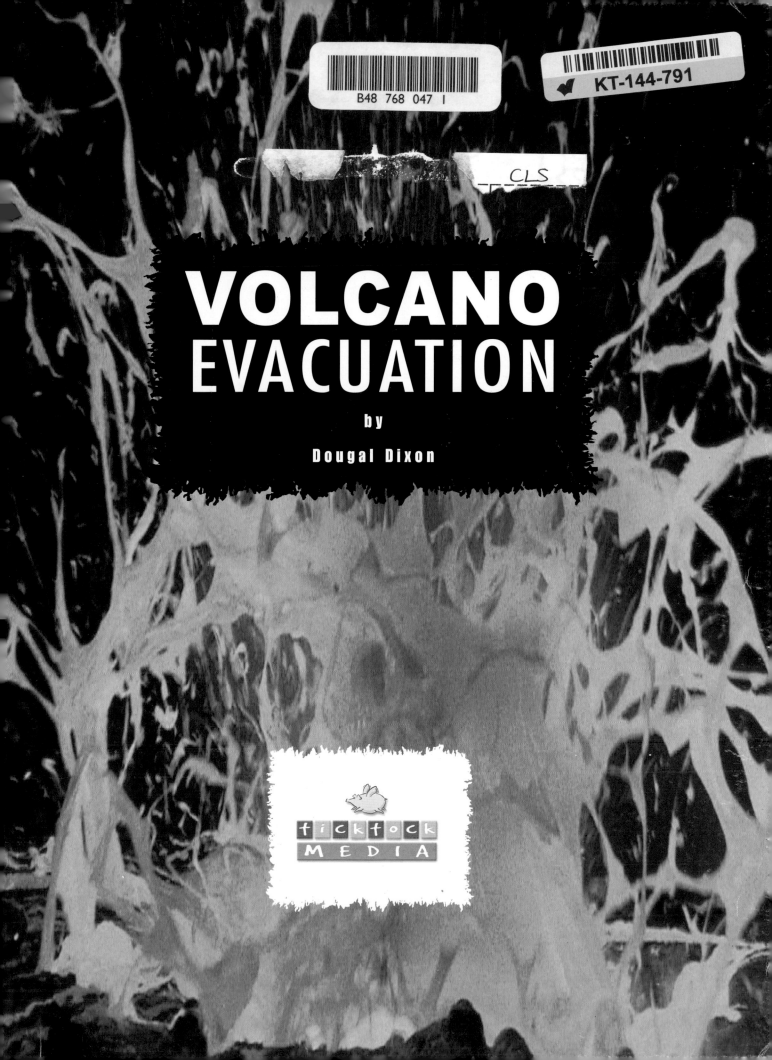

VOLCANO EVACUATION

by

Dougal Dixon

ticktock
MEDIA

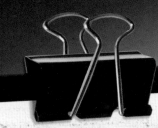

EXPEDITION EARTH
VOLCANO
EVACUATION

Dougal Dixon

Copyright © ticktock Entertainment Ltd 2004

First published in Great Britain in 2004 by ticktock Media Ltd.,

Unit 2, Orchard Business Centre, North Farm Road, Tunbridge Wells, Kent, TN2 3XF

We would like to thank: David Gillingwater and Elizabeth Wiggans

Illustrations by John Alston and David Gillingwater

ISBN 1 86007 436 7 hbk

ISBN 1 86007 432 4 pbk

Printed in China

A CIP catalogue record for this book is available from the British Library.

t=top, b=bottom, c=center, l=left, r=right, OFC=outside front cover, OBC=outside back cover

Alamy: 10-11c. Corbis: 12-13c, 16-17c, 22-23c, 24-25c, 28-29c, Creatas: 20-21.

Every effort has been made to trace the copyright holders, and we apologize in advance for any unintentional omissions.
We would be pleased to insert the appropriate acknowledgements in any subsequent edition of this publication.

CONTENTS

Paddy Robson

DAY 1
Location: *City School, Science Department*

Hi. I'm Paddy Robson, and I am crazy about volcanoes. This summer I am off to see a real volcano! Last week I was doing an interview for the school newspaper with a famous volcano expert at City University. I was asking the geologist specializing in vilcanology about his work as a vulcanologist when his telephone rang. It was another volcano expert asking him to go and look at a volcano that might be about to erupt. A day later he sent me a message asking me to join him! I am going to see volcanoes for myself!

I have to find out as much as I can about volcanoes before I go. It seems that there are two types of volcano. There are basaltic volcanoes that are quite gentle, and there are andesitic volcanoes that are the killers. I wonder which kind I am going to see...

Both Hawaii and Iceland are made up of basaltic volcanoes. I have always wanted to visit these amazing places.

GIANT'S CAUSEWAY
The Giant's Causeway in Northern Ireland is a basaltic lava flow that is 50 million years old. When the lava cooled, it cracked into these hexagonal columns.

DANTÉ'S PEAK

Here is a poster from my favorite film, *Dante's Peak*. It takes place around a rumbling volcano in the United States.

Cold basaltic lava is black and heavy, and it looks wrinkly. Vulcanologists call it *ropy pahoehoe*.

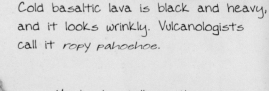

My books tell me these strange-looking rocks are called *breadcrust bombs*! They are fired out of erupting andesitic volcanoes.

BASALTIC VOLCANOES

A volcano is a mountain formed when molten rock from the earth's interior bursts out and solidifies on the surface. If the molten rock, called *lava*, is very runny, it will flow for a long distance before it cools and hardens. This forms a broad, low, shield-shaped volcano called a *basaltic volcano*. When the lava sets in lumpy blocks, geologists call it *aa lava*.

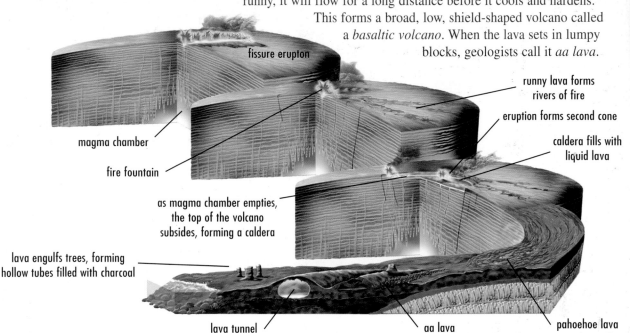

- fissure erupton
- runny lava forms rivers of fire
- eruption forms second cone
- magma chamber
- caldera fills with liquid lava
- fire fountain
- as magma chamber empties, the top of the volcano subsides, forming a caldera
- lava engulfs trees, forming hollow tubes filled with charcoal
- lava tunnel
- aa lava
- pahoehoe lava

ANDESITIC VOLCANOES

Sometimes, the molten rock is thick and stiff. When it breaks through the earth's surface, it throws out ashes and dust, or it forms a kind of lava that does not flow very far. The lava and ash build up steep-sided conical volcanoes called *andesitic volcanoes*. Sometimes, solidifying rock chokes the vent. When this happens, the pressure builds up below the vent until there is a very violent, explosive eruption.

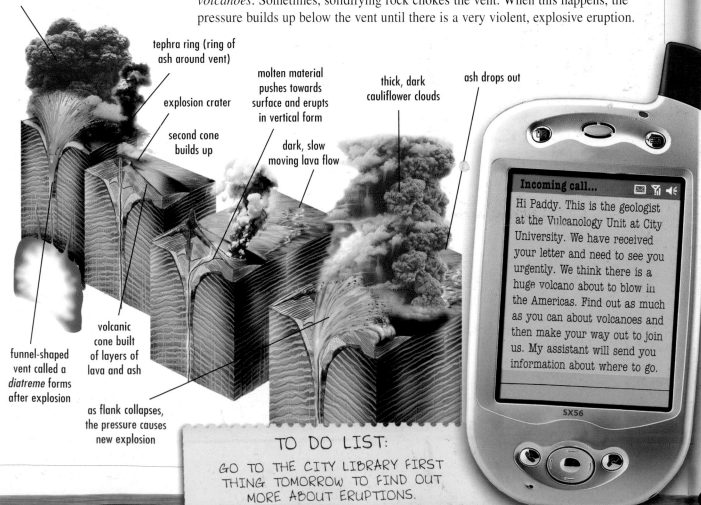

- Explosion of gas, ash, and dust
- tephra ring (ring of ash around vent)
- molten material pushes towards surface and erupts in vertical form
- thick, dark cauliflower clouds
- ash drops out
- explosion crater
- second cone builds up
- dark, slow moving lava flow
- volcanic cone built of layers of lava and ash
- funnel-shaped vent called a *diatreme* forms after explosion
- as flank collapses, the pressure causes new explosion

Incoming call...

Hi Paddy. This is the geologist at the Vulcanology Unit at City University. We have received your letter and need to see you urgently. We think there is a huge volcano about to blow in the Americas. Find out as much as you can about volcanoes and then make your way out to join us. My assistant will send you information about where to go.

SX56

TO DO LIST:

GO TO THE CITY LIBRARY FIRST THING TOMORROW TO FIND OUT MORE ABOUT ERUPTIONS.

DAY 2
Location: *The City Library*

I just hope we don't see anything like this! It must be terrifying!

I have been looking up stories of volcanic eruptions in the library. It seems that the lava of basaltic volcanoes does not have much of the element silica in it, and that is why it is runny. Basaltic eruptions are like spectacular glowing fountains and waterfalls of lava, and are usually tourist attractions. Andesitic eruptions, on the other hand, are horrible! Their lava is rich in silica, making it stiff and gooey. The volcanic pressure has to blast its way out.

In the library I found the most famous andesitic eruption of recent times. It was Mount Saint Helens in Washington State, USA in 1980. The United States Geological Survey (USGS) studied the eruption thoroughly – that is why I have been able to find so much information on it. It seems that Dr Firestone was there too, doing some work, a few months before the eruption.

U.S.G.S. - ACTIVITY REPORT
MOUNT ST HELENS ERUPTION

1972 Seismometers are installed near the volcano to measure underground tremors.

1975–1980 44 earthquakes recorded within a 22-mile area.

3/21/80 100 earthquakes are recorded in one week, including a huge earthquake on 3/20/80 that triggered snow avalanches.

3/25/80 Earthquakes increase to 20 per hour. The Federal Aviation Administration (F.A.A.) imposes flight restrictions over the mountain. A large crack appears in the snow on top of the mountain.

3/27/80 Following a loud boom, a large crater appears in the ice cap. A plume of black ash, smoke, and gas rises over 2,000 metres. The surrounding area is evacuated. Reservoirs in the area are emptied to accommodate mudflows and flooding from melting snow. Sulfur dioxide is detected in the gases, confirming that the magma in the volcano is reaching high temperatures.

4/11/80 A second crater appears. A huge bulge appears on the side of the mountain. It spreads 92 metres in just a few weeks. **A state of emergency is declared.** Tourists and volcano-watchers flock to the area.

5/17/80 Bulge is growing, but other activity stops.

5/18/80 8:32 A.M. Earthquake of magnitude 5.1 occurs. The bulge suddenly slides away in a gigantic avalanche, causing a huge release of pressure. The top 400 metres of the peak blasts off as a result. An avalanche of debris traveling 70–150 mph covers an area of 23 square miles. Mudslides, called *lahars*, pour down the mountain, causing an 255-metre-high tidal wave to sweep across Spirit Lake at the bottom of the mountain. The eruption cloud and the column of gas and ash rises 15 miles into the air. Pyroclastic flows (clouds of gas and ash) traveling at 50-80 mph cover the surrounding area. The temperature in the center of the clouds is 1,300 degrees Fahrenheit.

Incredibly, animals and plants began to return to the site only months after the eruption.

WILDLIFE RETURNS TO THE DEVASTATED SLOPES OF VOLCANO

When Mount St. Helens erupted in May 1980, it was estimated that over 7,000 elk, deer, and bears were killed in the initial blast. Thousands of smaller animals were killed by avalanches, and all birdlife in the area died. But now, just six months after these catastrophic events, life is returning to the mountain. Elk have been spotted throughout the area. Nature experts say that the elk will be vital to the recovery of the ecosystem. The elks' hooves will disturb the volcanic ash, uncovering the soil beneath. Their droppings will reintroduce nutrients and seeds to the mountain's slopes.

This is the geologist at Mount St. Helens in February 1980, just three months before the volcano erupted. The volcano had been dormant since 1857, and the peak is still intact.

The earth's outer surface is made up of individual sections called plates. We get andesitic eruptions, like the one that happened at Mount St. Helens, when the edges of these plates rub together. This usually happens in mountain chains and island arcs. If we look at a map of the earth's plates, we see that the shaded volcanic areas appear by the plate boundaries.

EARTH'S PLATE BOUNDARIES

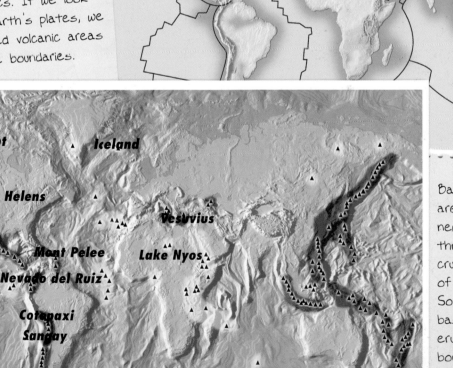

Redoubt • • Iceland

Mount Saint Helens

Hawaii

Vesuvius

Mont Pelee

Lake Nyos

Nevado del Ruiz

Cotapaxi

Sangay

Balsitic volcano
Andesitic volcano
▲ Active volcano

Basaltic volcanoes are formed when new material bursts through the earth's crust at the bottom of the ocean. Sometimes, though, basaltic volcanoes erupt far from plate boundaries, as in Hawaii and in Iceland.

DAY 3
Location: *The City Library*

Not many people were killed at Mount St Helens. That was because the mountain was so remote. But there have been many historical eruptions of andesitic volcanoes that have killed thousands of people. One of the most famous was the eruption of Vesuvius in AD 79, in which the towns of Pompeii, Herculaneum and Stabiae were destroyed. Sixteen-thousand people were killed that time.

I had always thought that the people of Pompeii had been killed by lava. I was wrong. It was the falling ash that killed them. It has been estimated that 4.13 cubic kilometres of rocky material rocketed out of Vesuvius in less than two days. Imagine all that engulfing the people of the city!

Vesuvius now has a rocky rim around its north side. This is the edge of the hole left by the eruption. Since then later eruptions have built up another volcanic cone at the peak.

It was the ash, not the lava, that killed people in Pompeii. It must have fallen from the sky or rolled down the hill, burying the whole city.

Vesuvius: A History

The Roman writer Pliny witnessed the eruption from across the Bay of Naples. In his writing, Pliny said, "[The great cloud] looked like an umbrella pine tree. It was daylight everywhere else by this time, but they [the people of Strabiae] were still enveloped in a darkness that was blacker than any night."

Pliny lost his uncle in a rescue mission. He described the tragedy in harrowing detail, saying, "He suffocated when the dense fumes choked him . . . looking more like a man asleep than dead."

Since 79 A.D., there have been many eruptions of Vesuvius, the most serious occuring in 472 and 1631 A.D.

THE POMPEII ERUPTION

A FAMOUS DISASTER

The architecture of Pompeii has been preserved in time. The eruption caused little structural damage to the buildings, but the fall of ash buried them, entombing them for 17 centuries. The site was rediscovered in 1748, and a systematic excavation has carried on there ever since. Archaeological digs have revealed the layout of a whole Roman city buried under the fallen ash fall at Pompeii. All types of structures, from theaters to toilets, have been preserved. The whole site provides a detailed look at life in Roman times.

NATURAL DISASTERS

These are counters in Pompeiian food shops. They would have held pots of food or wine.

Archaeologists have uncovered the grisly remains of many of Pompeii's inhabitants. Those who died, suffocated by the dust and cinders, lay buried for centuries. Their bodies decayed away, leaving hollows in the solidified ash. Excavators have filled these hollows with plaster of Paris, producing casts of the people lying in the positions in which they died.

Incoming call...

Hi, Paddy. This is the geologist's assistant. Catch Flight 247 to the Pacific coast. The team will be there to meet you and bring you to Upper Village near the volcano. They will update you on what we have found so far.

SX56

DAY 4
Location: *Pacific Coast Airport*

I have just flown into the capital of the region. Like most countries along the Pacific coast of the Americas, the area is a mountainous place with volcanoes. It looks as if all the volcanoes here are the andesitic type rather than the gentle basaltic type. This could be dangerous.

The members of the Doctor's team met me at the airport, and for the last six hours we have been bounced about in a four-wheel drive vehicle, along dusty mountain roads until at last we are in Upper Town. The town is just beneath the volcano. The volcano looks very sinister. It has steep sides with a steaming peak set inside a huge caldera. Like at Vesuvius, this caldera was formed when the peak collapsed during a huge eruption centuries ago. I keep thinking about all those poor people in Pompeii...

VOLCANOES RUMBLE

All along the Pacific coast of the Americas, volcanoes are constantly rumbling away. This year, two volcanoes have been threatening to erupt. All countries on the east coast of the Americas have their own unstable volcanoes. This is where the Pacific plate is grinding down beneath the continents.

Cut out from *The Volcano*,
July 23, 2003

The Earth Science Student *is specialising in the internal workings of andesitic volcanoes (she calls it "the plumbing"). She has worked with the team before in the Philippines and in Japan.*

The Photographer's *speciality is taking photographs of volcanoes from dangerous angles. He has no formal qualifications in vulcanology, but he has learned a great deal from this hobby.*

The Geologist *is a lecturer in geology. He has made a career out of studying volcanoes in the region, particularly the one we have come to monitor. He is our local guide.*

The Meteorologist *is studying the movement of volcanic ash through the atmosphere. She became hooked on the subject as a child when her father's tourist shop in Iceland was buried by an ash fall.*

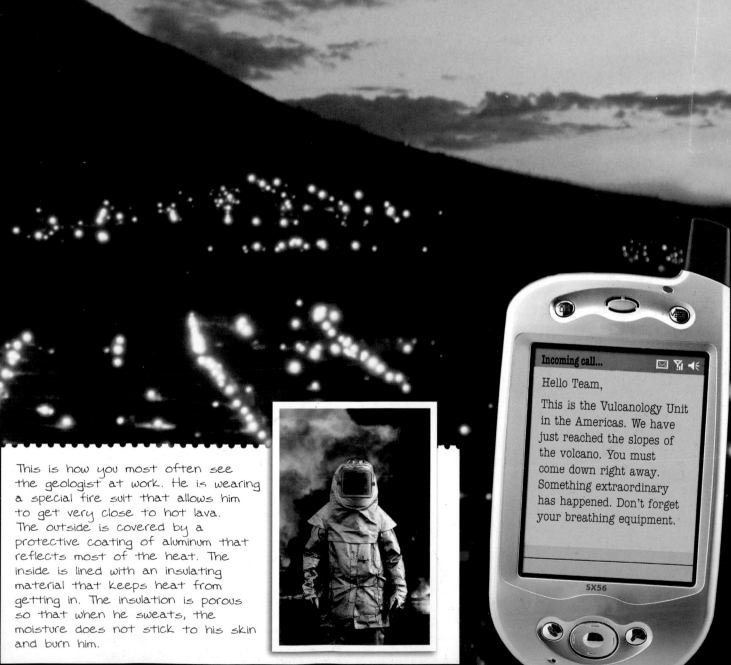

This is how you most often see the geologist at work. He is wearing a special fire suit that allows him to get very close to hot lava. The outside is covered by a protective coating of aluminum that reflects most of the heat. The inside is lined with an insulating material that keeps heat from getting in. The insulation is porous so that when he sweats, the moisture does not stick to his skin and burn him.

Incoming call...

Hello Team,

This is the Vulcanology Unit in the Americas. We have just reached the slopes of the volcano. You must come down right away. Something extraordinary has happened. Don't forget your breathing equipment.

SX56

DAY 5
Location: *Poisoned Farm, south slope of the volcano*

This is what we came to see, and what a sight it is! Dozens of dead cows in a gully. We weren't allowed to get too close, but the scene looked just like this tragic photograph taken at Lake Nyos in Cameroon some years ago. They are beginning to smell a bit now, but apparently when it happened it looked as if they had just lain down to sleep. It is just how Pliny described the death of his uncle all those years ago at Vesuvius.

Two university colleagues of the Doctor's are already there. They think that the tragedy was caused by an eruption of gas from the old crater lake at the head of the gully.

It has been over 40 years since the volcano last erupted. People thought it was safe to settle here, raise livestock and plant coffee and vines. The farmer is distraught at the loss of his cows. But imagine if he or his family had been in the gully when it happened...

CARBON DIOXIDE
Carbon dioxide is one of the most common volcanic gases. It is heavier than air, so if it is present in large quantities, it tends to stay close to the ground. If you inhale a lot of carbon dioxide, you will suffocate because you cannot get enough oxygen into your system. Carbon dioxide is soluble in water. In fact, it is the gas that makes the bubbles in soft drinks. Sometimes, if the conditions of the water change, carbon dioxide can come fizzing out. The team thinks that this is what happened here at the farm.

The poisoned farm we are visiting is in a bad location. Directly above it is a lake that was formed by a small crater that was filled with water a long time ago. The carbon dioxide seeping up through the volcano has been dissolving in this water for years. Now, as the volcano seems to have increased in activity, the carbon dioxide has fizzed out of the lake. It pours down the mountainside, poisoning anything that gets in its way.

Sketch of the area drawn by the geologist

N

Volcano

Crater lake

The poisoned farm

Upper Town

Steep slope of ash cone

River

River

Lower Town

DISASTER
AT LAKE NYOS

VOLCANO TERROR HITS TOWN

Lake Nyos in Cameroon was the site, yesterday, of an eruption of carbon dioxide gas from the water of the volcanic crater. For about 15 to 20 seconds there was a loud rumbling as a huge cloud of gas gushed upward into the air over 80 metres above the crater rim. It then fell back to earth and poured down the mountainside at speeds of up to 30 mph, suffocating everything as it went. In the hospital at Subum, 6 miles downhill, patients on the second floor survived, but those on the ground floor suffocated. It is estimated that 1,700 people and 3,000 livestock have perished.

Cut out from *The Volcano*, August 21, 1986

MONITORING THE VOLCANO

DAY 6
Location: *Volcano summit*

I am up here at the summit, and the team is setting out all the equipment to test if the volcano is about to erupt. They are putting out instruments to test the temperature and sample the gases. They also have meters that measure if the tilt of the mountain is changing. Seismometers will detect any earth tremors that would accompany an eruption.

The first results are in already. They say that the increase in sulphur dioxide that they are detecting in the gases (they hardly need an instrument – it smells like rotten eggs everywhere) means that there is magma rising from deep below. Magma is the molten rock that becomes lava as it reaches the surface. They are also finding that the mountain is tilting, being pushed up from beneath. Temperatures are rising too. That is not a good sign.

I don't think they need the equipment. I can almost feel it happening!

Volcano slopes

Note: The V.D.A.P. (Volcano Disaster Assistance Program) was successful in predicting the eruption of Pinatubo in 1991.

USGS
Mobile Response Team Saves Lives in Volcano Crises

The U.S. Geological Survey (U.S.G.S) handed out to people living in areas at risk of volcano damage. It tells people what to do in the event of an emergency.

Note: You may want to visit the U.S.G.S. website. It is packed with a lot of valuable information: www.usgs.gov

This is a seismometer. The team uses this instrument to measure vibrations around the volcano. If they detect any vibrations, an eruption could be on the way.

Steam and gas are hissing out of the cone. Bits of ash are being pushed out and are rattling down the side of the mountain. It makes an eerie metallic clinking noise like trains shifting tracks.

Volcano summit

Crater Lake

This is a tiltmeter. Our team is using one to monitor the changing shape of a volcanic mountain to predict an eruption. The readings they are getting show the volcano is starting to bulge.

This is a gas analyzer. It is used to alert! vulcanologists to carbon dioxide coming out of the volcano. This might have been responsible for killing all those cattle at the farm we visited.

This is a digital thermometer. Because it can withstand very high temperatures, it can be used to determine how hot the volcano becomes. It can also give the geologist an idea of whether or not it may erupt.

PLATINUM RTD

27.9

OFF ON °C °F

MINCO   TI142
DIGITAL THERMOMETER

Ipex 1

DAY 7
Location: *Upper Town*

The results are coming in. And it does not look good! With the information the team is able to plot a hazard map, showing what might happen when the volcano erupts. There will be a fall of ash. There may be pyroclastic flows – mixtures of white-hot ash and expanding gas that flow downhill like water. There may be lahars – mud flows caused by rain mixing with newly-fallen ash. The hazard map shows where these might take place, and how likely they are.

Upper Town is in a very dangerous position – being directly downhill from the lowest point of the caldera rim. The team wants the town evacuated, but the mayor is not keen. It is election year and he does not want to spread panic. He has agreed to issue a "yellow alert". This means that the townspeople are made aware that there might be a problem and urged to move their belongings out.

SATELLITE IMAGE
We have just received a satellite image beamed down from the university. Satellites have been monitoring the mountain over the years and have noticed that the peak is being pushed up from below by rising magma. The changes in height are shown by different computer generated colours. The red areas are where the ground has been pushed up the most.

The geologist showed me how a pyroclastic flow works. It is like shaking a soft drink bottle and then releasing the pressure. Instead of soda, white-hot lava shoots out. Instead of carbon dioxide bubbles, expanding, scalding gases are released.

HAZARD MAP

The hazard map is used to plot the likelihood of damage from an eruption. If anything erupts, it will flow downhill. From their experience, the photographer and the geologist have plotted how far pyroclastic flows are likely to run and in which direction. The earth science expert has determined where lahars would cause the most damage along the rivers. The meteorologist has been estimating, from the prevailing winds, where we are likely to get deep falls of ash. These are all serious hazards. Putting all this together, it looks as if Upper Town and Lower Town are in the worst possible positions.

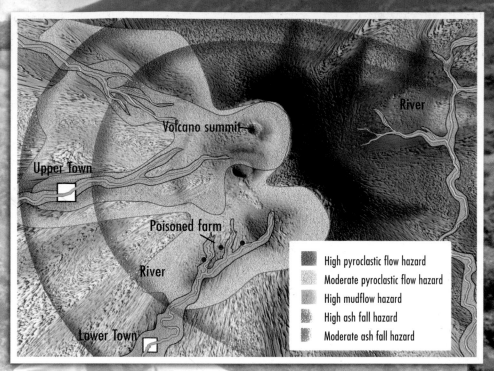

River

Volcano summit

Upper Town

Poisoned farm

River

Lower Town

High pyroclastic flow hazard

Moderate pyroclastic flow hazard

High mudflow hazard

High ash fall hazard

Moderate ash fall hazard

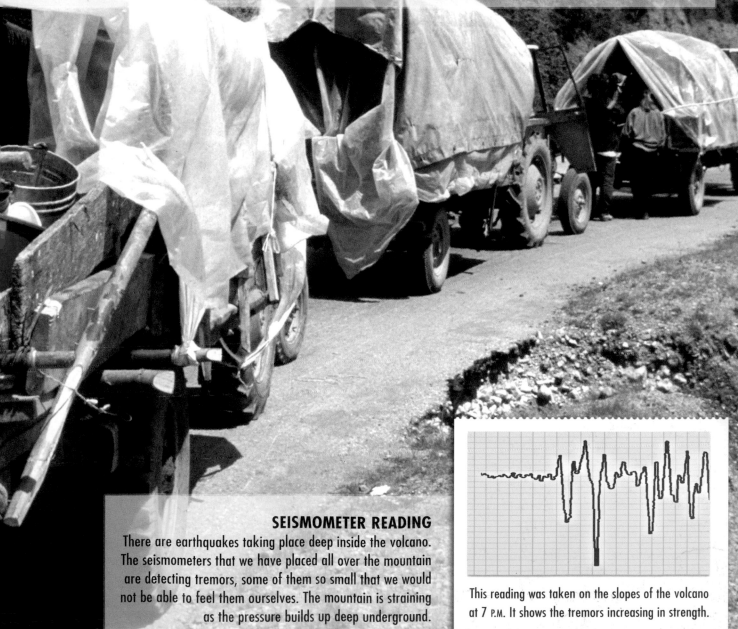

SEISMOMETER READING

There are earthquakes taking place deep inside the volcano. The seismometers that we have placed all over the mountain are detecting tremors, some of them so small that we would not be able to feel them ourselves. The mountain is straining as the pressure builds up deep underground.

This reading was taken on the slopes of the volcano at 7 P.M. It shows the tremors increasing in strength.

DAY 8
Location: *The hills above Upper Town*

There it goes! At about 8 a.m. there was a shaking that brought plaster from the adobe walls, followed by a distant rumbling, like thunder. A complete forest right by the volcano was totally flattened by the blast. We left our breakfasts and ran out on to the cobbled street to see the column of ash roiling up into the sky from the summit of the volcano. Live images are being fed back to my laptop and the action looks explosive.

We have moved to the high ground on the ridge to the north of the town. All day the ash column – all knobbly like a cauliflower head, but filthy – has risen far into the sky. The meteorology expert reckons it is about six miles high now. It is spreading out as it hits different layers of the atmosphere. This must be what Pliny meant when he talked about the smoke from Vesuvius being "like a pine tree".

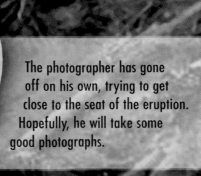

The photographer has gone off on his own, trying to get close to the seat of the eruption. Hopefully, he will take some good photographs.

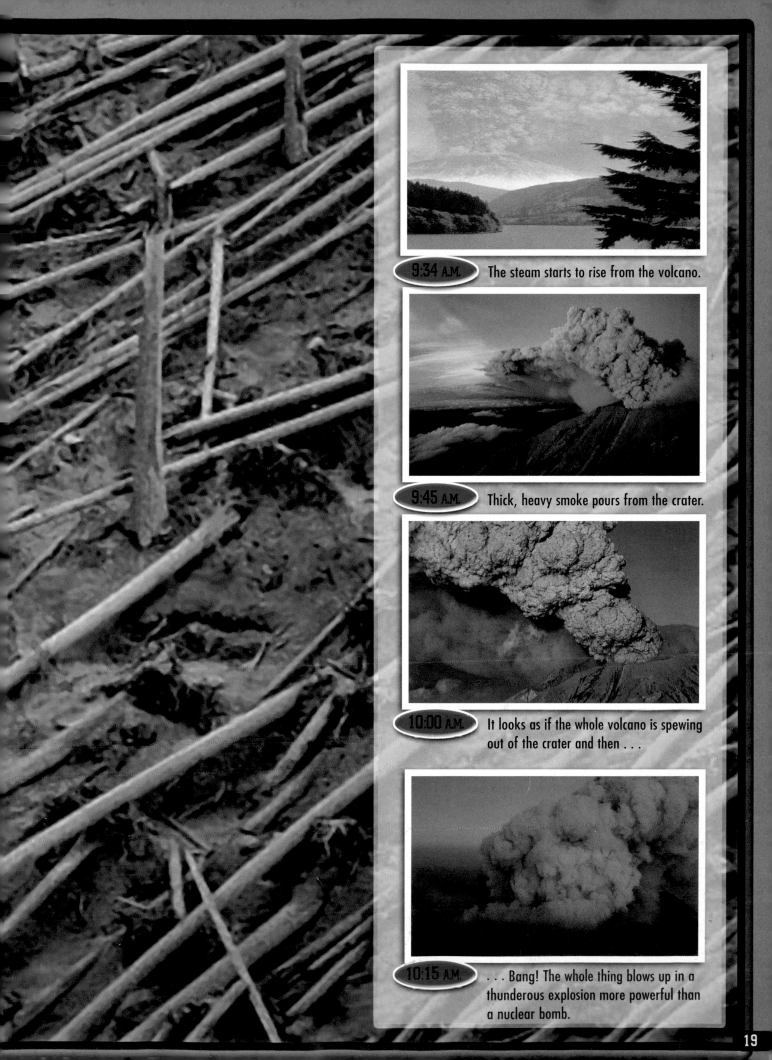

9:34 A.M. The steam starts to rise from the volcano.

9:45 A.M. Thick, heavy smoke pours from the crater.

10:00 A.M. It looks as if the whole volcano is spewing out of the crater and then . . .

10:15 A.M. . . . Bang! The whole thing blows up in a thunderous explosion more powerful than a nuclear bomb.

DAY 9

Location: *The hills above Upper Town*

It was 4.08 p.m. when Upper Town died. I did not really comprehend what a pyroclastic flow entailed. The Doctor talked about hot ash and expanding gas, but I never imagined anything as horrible as this. People on the ridge became excited and started pointing. We looked up from our temporary camp and watched as the whole mountain was hidden by what looked like a curtain of roiling ash sweeping down the valley. And it was silent! No rumbles or explosions that you would normally associate with cataclysmic destruction – just a distant hissing and clinking sound. It rolled by, flowing with the speed of running water, beating us with a blast of hot air as it passed showing that deep inside the blackness the mass was white hot. It totally engulfed Upper Town. I do hope that everybody was able to get out...

This is a picture of Martinique after it was hit by a eruption. Upper Town looks just like this now.

DISASTER HITS MARTINIQUE

On May 8, 1902, Mont Pelée on the island of Martinique erupted. It sent a mass of ash and cinders, lubricated by expanding searingly hot gas, down the valleys and into the unsuspecting town of St. Pierre. Around 29,000 people perished within seconds, having no time to escape. The build-up of pressure within the mountain had been released as the peak collapsed, and the pressurized gas suddenly expanded. The mass of white-hot gas and ash poured freely downhill in a phenomenon known as a *nuée ardente*—a "glowing cloud." Nowadays, vulcanologists call this a *pyroclastic flow*.

The damage from the blast is just incredible. Anything in the way of the hot ash has been destroyed, including cars, houses, and office buildings.

DAY 10
Location: *On the edge of Upper Town*

The sky is black with dust – just as Pliny described. Nobody can get back into the town yet. Most of it is buried in ash, and it is still too hot. Not that there will be much to go back to. It probably will not be worthwhile rebuilding Upper Town. If the ash of the pyroclastic flow has settled on the town it will have fused into a solid mass before it cooled. The earth science specialist reckons that a volcano like this will keep on erupting for the next 20 months.

It is most uncomfortable. We cannot breathe properly because of the floating ash. We have to cover our faces with bandanas. The meterology expert had spare shower caps in her kit and so we are wearing them. We look silly but it keeps the ash out of our hair. To make it worse, the rain has started.

L A V A   F L O W

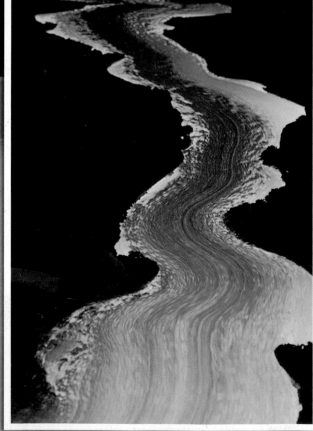

A DIFFERENT ERUPTION

My aunt went to Hawaii last year and saw a basaltic eruption. She sent back photographs of it. That is what I thought I was going to witness here, instead of the choking, dusty horror that surrounds me now. There is a big difference between a basaltic eruption and an andesitic one.

BASALTIC LAVA FLOW

Basaltic lava flows in glowing rivers, not in grey, dusty clouds. An andesitic lava flow on the other hand, when not tumbling in a pyroclastic flow, is more like a steaming pile of ash being pushed along slowly.

The drifting ash may look soft like snow, but it is not. It consists of tiny, spiky shards like powdered glass. It irritates the eyes, dries out the throat, and chokes the lungs.

Buildings catch fire as basaltic lava flows around them, although there is little threat to human life. An andesitic pyroclastic flow kills as well as destroys.

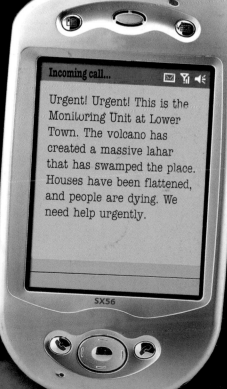

Incoming call...

Urgent! Urgent! This is the Monitoring Unit at Lower Town. The volcano has created a massive lahar that has swamped the place. Houses have been flattened, and people are dying. We need help urgently.

SX56

SOLID FLOW (OR PAHOEHOE)

Solidified basalt often has a wrinkly surface and is known by its Hawaiian name of *pahoehoe*. Sometimes the flow is more turbulent, and it solidifies with a blocky surface, similar to solidified andesitic lava. This is called *aa* (pronounced ah-ah).

DAY 10 (Evening)
Location: *Lower Town*

You don't think of mud as being very dangerous — slimy wet stuff that forms in a puddle — hardly something that could kill you.

But when you get mud in these quantities, it can wipe out whole towns. It has been raining all night. Water vapour makes up a big proportion of volcanic gas, and this has been falling as rain. It has mixed with the freshly-fallen ash, and the resulting slurry has been pouring off the hills. Where it gets channelled into river valleys it forms a destructive flow known by its Javanese name lahar. (Many geological phenomena are known by the names given to them in the places they occur. Look at aa and pahoehoe - both found in Hawaii and both given native names.)

Lower Town was unlucky enough to be sited in a river valley, and has borne the full force of a slithering, pouring, engulfing mass of liquid mud. The possibility did show up on our hazard map.

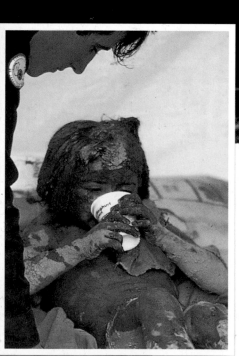

The survivors of the mudflow are exhausted. Imagine being up to your neck in clinging mud and trying to pull your way through it. Then, if you are not lucky enough to pull yourself free before it dries out under the hot sun, it will set like concrete and entomb you. Some survivors here were carried along on rafts of debris, and they escaped.

Japan builds dams to protect its villages from lahars. Huge steel frameworks trap the rocks and treetrunks that are carried along by mudflows. These build up into solid barriers that deflect the flow of the mud. Japan is a rich nation and can afford to do this. The Pacific coastal country we are in is not.

This tragedy in Colombia happened nearly 20 years ago. It was very similar to our volcanic eruption.

DISASTER
AT NEVADO DEL RUIS

A minor volcanic eruption in Colombia yesterday caused a major disaster. The 5,500 metre volcano Nevado del Ruiz threw up a fountain of hot ash that landed on the glaciers of the mountain peak. The ice melted and mixed with the ash, forming lahars that flowed downhill into the surrounding valleys.

The greatest loss of life was in the town of Armero to the east, by the mouth of one of the valleys. Two hours after the eruption, a 43 metre wave of mud spread out into the town, killing 21,000 people. Another 1,000 died in the surrounding areas.

Back in September, an eruption melted part of the ice cap, but the warnings of that event do not seem to have been heeded.

The village must have received some warning. All the children in the school had time to climb onto the roof and are now awaiting rescue. Luckily, their building did not collapse as other buildings in Lower Town did.

Liquid mud swept fallen treetrunks through like battering rams, smashing away the foundations of the wooden houses.

Cut out from *The Volcano*, August 14, 1986

DAY 10 (Evening)
Location: *Camp above the remains of Upper Town*

At last, the rescue operation seems to be under way. It has taken some time for the relief operation to be started. The main problem is the amount of dust still in the sky. You cannot fly aeroplanes through dust-laden atmosphere or their engines will fail. Now, however, helicopters are bringing in tents and shelters as temporary housing for the survivors of Upper and Lower Town.

We don't know how many people have been killed yet, but it looks as if most were able to get out. There is no sign of the mayor of San Jorge. Nobody knows if he stayed in the town because he thought that nothing was going to happen, or if he has run away because he made the wrong decisions and does not want to face the consequences.

At least the cameraman has come back to us. He has spent the last few days photographing the disaster from all angles.

Extent of pyroclastic flow
Extent of mudflow
Depth of ash flow (in)

Volcano
Crater lake
20
16
12
8

Now we can see the extent of the damage. A pyroclastic flow destroyed Upper Town, while a lahar destroyed Lower Town. The whole countryside is covered by a deep layer of ash, destroying crops and livestock.

BOEING ALMOST DOWNED OVER VOLCANO

Earlier this month, a KLM Boeing 747 flew into the ash cloud from Redoubt volcano in Alaska. One after the other, the four engines failed, clogged by dust. The aircraft fell 4,000 metres in eight minutes before the crew managed to restart the engines and make an emergency landing at Anchorage. No one was hurt.

Cut out from *The Volcano*, December 29, 1989

Flights to the area have been suspended because of what happened over ten years ago. Volcanic ash nearly brought a plane down.

The International Red Cross and Red Crescent are flying in supplies for the survivors.

Trucks and llamas have been bringing food up the mountain tracks ever since the eruptions started. At last, they have arrived, and the aid is being distributed.

Drinking water is in high demand. Most of the wells are clogged, and all of the water systems have collapsed.

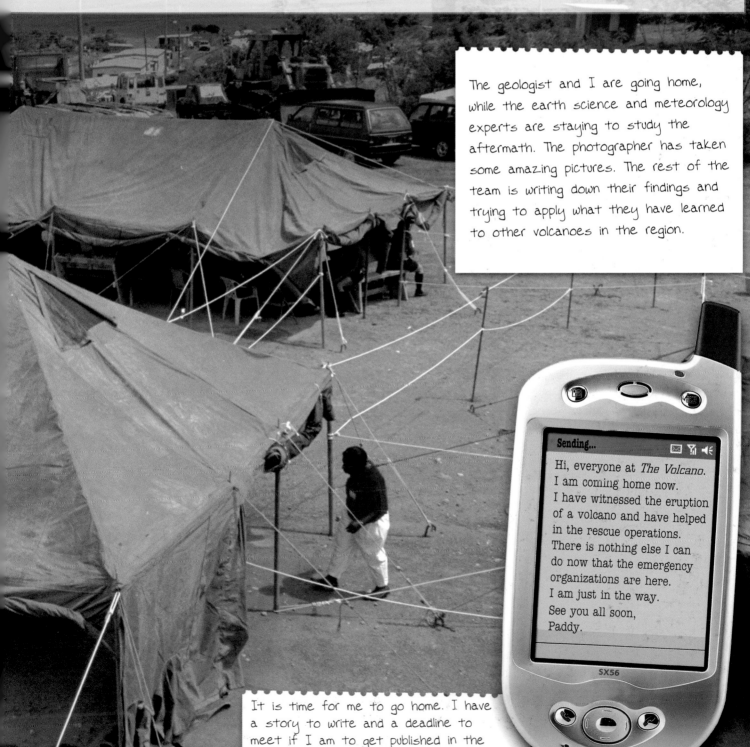

The geologist and I are going home, while the earth science and meteorology experts are staying to study the aftermath. The photographer has taken some amazing pictures. The rest of the team is writing down their findings and trying to apply what they have learned to other volcanoes in the region.

Sending...

Hi, everyone at *The Volcano*. I am coming home now. I have witnessed the eruption of a volcano and have helped in the rescue operations. There is nothing else I can do now that the emergency organizations are here. I am just in the way. See you all soon, Paddy.

It is time for me to go home. I have a story to write and a deadline to meet if I am to get published in the next issue of *The Volcano*.

Three years later, I received a request to write an update on Upper Town. As you can see, the town has started to pick itself up again.

A TOWN RECOVERS

A look at the mountain and surrounding landscape in the aftermath of the eruption. With a special report by our junior reporter from the City School.

It has been three years since I witnessed the terrible eruption at Upper Town. I have returned with the memory of the terrible destruction caused by the pyroclastic flow, the lahars, and the suffocating blanket of gray ash that covered the entire landscape. I have found that those who survived are managing to put their lives back together.

Upper Town has been rebuilt in a new location. It is now located higher up on the ridge. Although pyroclastic flows have been known to build up enough speed to sweep uphill over ridges and plunge into valleys, the new site of the town should be safe from the worst danger.

Lower Town has sprung up again on its old site. Now, there is a complex arrangement of dams and barriers upstream that should divert any lahars that are likely to threaten the town again. An international assistance program was able to raise the money for these dams and barriers. A team from the Volcano Disaster Assistance Program has now placed monitors-tilt meters, seismometers, gas detectors, and temperature gauges-all over the mountain. Their readings are constantly relayed by satellite to the

Botanists measure the growth of new plants on the upper reaches of the volcano.

A symbol of regeneration. This coconut germinates on the beach of volcanic sand.

newly-opened volcanic institute nearby. The area will never be as vulnerable as it was three years ago. What surprised me the most, though, was how green the mountainside had become. When I left, it was bleak and grey, shrouded in ash. Now, the coffee plantations and the vineyards have been replanted, and the local economy will soon be back to where it was.

One unexpected side effect of the eruption is that the ash fall has refertilized the local soil, so the crops are growing more bountifully than ever. This is hardly surprising. Frequent volcanic eruptions are a fact of life in these areas. In the last three years, two other volcanoes in the region have erupted, although not as violently.

Volcanoes used to be classified as active, dormant, or extinct. Either they were erupting, they were expected to erupt sometime, or they

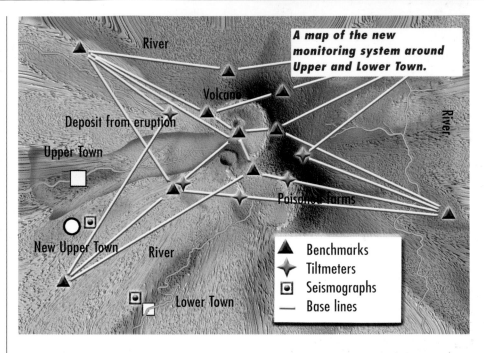

A map of the new monitoring system around Upper and Lower Town.

River

Volcano

Deposit from eruption

Upper Town

New Upper Town

River

Poison farms

River

Lower Town

▲ Benchmarks
✦ Tiltmeters
▣ Seismographs
— Base lines

would never erupt again. In historical times, so many "extinct" volcanoes have suddenly and surprisingly erupted. As a result, the classification has been changed. Now, volcanoes are classified as active or inactive.

Disasters are always catching us

by surprise. Although it is important to stay alert, it is also important to remember that life here has always adapted to meet a changing environment. One thing is for certain. Life and the environment will continue to change in the future.

Black sand on a Pacific shoreline. This is volcanic ash brought all the way down from volcanoes by rivers. The coastline around Upper and Lower Town now looks similar to this.

GLOSSARY

Aa A flow of lava that solidifies with a broken blocky surface.

Andesitic A type of lava or a volcano that contains a large amount of the element silica in its chemical makeup. Andesitic lava, called *andesite*, is stiff, does not flow very far, and builds up steep-sided volcanoes.

Archaeologist A scientist who studies ancient people and civilizations by digging up their remains.

Basaltic A type of lava or a volcano having a low proportion of the element silica in its chemical makeup. A basaltic lava, called *basalt*, is runny and flows for long distances, building up low volcanoes.

Baseline In surveying, it is a line that serves as a basis for measuring.

Bench mark In surveying, it is a place above sea level or a distance from a known place that serves as a point of reference. Measurements can be made against this point.

Bomb In vulcanology, it is a lump of molten material thrown out of a volcano that solidifies in the air before it falls.

Crater A huge hole in a volcano that is formed when a magma chamber becomes empty, causing the peak to collapse.

Diatreme A funnel-shaped vent in the crust of the earth that is formed as magma under pressure blasts its way to the surface.

Dormant A volcano that is not currently erupting but may erupt in the future.

Earthquake A movement of the earth, either caused by the earth's plates sliding by one another or by the action of erupting volcanoes.

Erupt To burst out at the surface.

Fire fountain A fountain of basaltic lava flung high into the air by the pressure of the eruption.

Geology The study of the earth.

Hexagonal Having six sides.

Lahar A flow of mud formed when loose volcanic ash mixes with water and flows downhill. The word is Javanese.

Lava Molten rock that erupts at the surface of the earth. The term is often used to describe the kind of solid rock that forms as it cools.

Lava tunnel A natural cave formed by a lava flow. As lava, particularly basaltic lava, flows, the outside cools and solidifies while the molten material still flows within. The molten lava may pour away, leaving the solid roof and sides as a tunnel.

Magma Molten rocky material below the earth's surface. When it erupts at the surface, it becomes lava.

Magma chamber A region below the earth's surface where magma gathers. Volcanoes usually form where magma pushes its way upward from a magma chamber.

Meteorology The study of the atmosphere, its movements, and the climates and weather that it causes.

Nuée ardente An old name for a pyroclastic flow. It is French for "glowing cloud."

Pahoehoe A flow of lava that solidifies with a wrinkled ropy-looking surface.

Plate In geology, it is a section of the outermost part of the earth's structure. A plate consists of the earth's crust and top part of the mantle. Earthquakes and volcanoes occur where plates meet and move in different directions. The outside of the earth is made up of less than a dozen plates.

Pyroclastic flow A mixture of white-hot ash and lava, newly erupted from a volcano. It is filled with expanding gas bubbles and flows rapidly downhill from the eruption.

Satellite An instrument in orbit around the earth. It may carry sensors that examine the ground surface immediately below. It may contain communications devices for sending messages. Or, it may contain both.

Seismograph An instrument that detects earthquakes and prints out or displays a reading.

Seismometer An instrument that measures ground movement during an earthquake.

Silica One of the most common elements in the minerals and rocks of the earth.

Tephra A term for solid matter that erupts from a volcano, including ash, dust, and bombs.

Tiltmeter An instrument used for measuring the tilt of the ground and how it changes.

Tremor A small earthquake.

Volcano A mountain formed as molten magma erupts at the surface of the earth. It usually forms a cone-shaped hill built up from successive layers of tephra or lava.

Vulcanology The study of volcanoes.

INDEX